Arabia after the Storm: Internal Stability of the Gulf Arab States

ROGER HARDY

A MIDDLE EAST PROGRAMME REPORT

© Royal Institute of International Affairs, 1992

First published in Great Britain in 1992 by the Royal Institute of International Affairs, Chatham House, 10 St James's Square, London SW1Y 4LE.

Registered Charity Number 208223

ISBN 0 905031 51 2

Printed and bound in Great Britain by the Chameleon Press Ltd

Ordering details

Copies may be ordered direct from either the Middle East Programme or the Publications Department at: The Royal Institute of International Affairs
Chatham House, 10 St James's Square, London SW1Y 4LE.

Telephone: 071 957 5700, Fax: 071 957 5710. Price: £10.00. Please remember to add a postage charge of £1.50 for within Europe or £3.50 for outside Europe.

CONTENTS

TABLES

FOREWORD

This report is the third publication in a short series which focuses on the Gulf in the wake of the 1990/91 crisis. It follows Richard Dalton's study on Gulf security, entitled *Winning Peace in the Gulf: A Long-Term View*, and Paul Stevens' study on Gulf energy, entitled *Oil and Politics: The Post-War Gulf*, which were published in April and September 1992 respectively.

In this report Roger Hardy assesses the domestic impact of the Gulf crisis on the six states of the Gulf Cooperation Council. He argues that the crisis has generated pressures for change which the ruling families will find difficult to accommodate. In particular, he points to the demands from both liberals and Islamists for greater accountability, managerial competence and political participation in the Gulf states. These demands, he believes, are likely to increase as a younger, better educated and more populous generation emerges on the scene.

The Programme is grateful for the financial support for its work on the post crisis Gulf to the Mitsubishi Research Institute of Japan, in particular Noriko Hama of their London office, and Johsin Takehashi and Yasuo Sato in Tokyo. Special thanks must also go to our regular supporters for their generous support since the Programme's inception, particularly British Aerospace, Shell, BP and Mobil.

More generally, the Middle East Programme expects to bring out a number of new publications towards the beginning of next year. A major book on Israel's domestic challenges, edited by Keith Kyle and Joel Peters, is to be published by I.B. Tauris. Sarah Collinson's book on migration, to be published in conjunction with Pinter, is close to completion. A Middle East Programme report on EC-Arab World economic relations is being prepared by Mina Toksoz. A second, revised and updated edition of Richard Schofield's definitive work on the Iraq-Kuwait territorial dispute has been completed. Work will soon begin on two additional reports in the EC-Arabs series, to focus on security and political relations. It is hoped soon to initiate new research projects on: Turkish foreign policy; the multilaterals and the peace process; migration policy in North Africa; and asset freezing.

Dr Philip Robins
Director, Middle East Programme
RIIA

November 1992

ACKNOWLEDGMENTS

In preparing this report, I have benefited from the comments of a number of Gulf Arabs who agreed to be interviewed, and a wide range of specialists – journalists, academics, businessmen, and others – who responded patiently to my questions.

Nicholas Van Hear, of the Refugee Studies Programme in Oxford, pointed me to useful sources on migrant workers.

J.E. Peterson kindly read the manuscript and made a number of helpful comments.

A study group at Chatham House in March 1992 provided food for thought. Finally the staff of the Middle East Programme at Chatham House – particularly Philip Robins and Jill Kalawoun – have been helpful at every stage.

None of these individuals, however, are responsible for the opinions expressed in this report; nor should they be attributed either to the Royal Institute of International Affairs or to the BBC. The responsibility is mine alone.

November 1992

Roger Hardy
BBC World Service

INTRODUCTION

It requires an effort of the imagination now, more than two years after Iraq's invasion of Kuwait, to recall the sound and fury of Operation Desert Storm. Like many wars, it seemed a turning-point. How many times did we hear that the Middle East would never be the same again? The war, like all wars, generated great hopes and fears. There were confident predictions that, once the fighting was over, the Arabian oligarchies would have to share power with their peoples, give their foreign workers a new deal, and work out a new and fairer relationship with the rest of the Arab world. The Gulf rulers themselves seem to have been infected by the mood:

> 'Saddam has exploded our fantasy culture,' says a senior Gulf official, seated
> in a palace of marbled halls and Persian carpets. 'A wealthy island in a sea of
> poverty cannot live securely forever.'[1]

All this rings hollow now. A six-month crisis culminated in a war so short (42 days, the ground war a mere 100 hours) that the shock wore off quickly. The Gulf rulers and their peoples sighed with relief – and went back to business as usual. Democracy and freedom of expression have not broken out. Foreign workers are treated no better than they were. The Gulf Arabs seem less, rather than more, inclined to share their wealth with the Arab poor. The 'fantasy culture' is alive and well.

But it would be facile to assume that the war changed nothing. It ended, for the time being, Iraq's pretensions to regional supremacy. It split the Arab world in two. It gave new impetus to the search for Arab–Israeli peace. These are among the visible effects of the war; others are subterranean.

In the six states of the Gulf Co-operation Council (GCC: Saudi Arabia, Kuwait, Bahrain, Qatar, the United Arab Emirates and Oman) which are the focus of this report, the crisis generated pressures and tensions which have not disappeared. In Saudi Arabia it provoked an Islamic backlash (chapter 3), in the lower Gulf an undercurrent of dissent

---

[1] Geraldine Brooks and Tony Horwitz, 'However Crisis in Gulf Plays Out, Arab Chiefs Face a Changed World',
Wall Street Journal (European edition), 2 January 1991.

(chapter 4), in Kuwait a crisis of confidence for the ruling Al Sabah family (chapter 5). The war highlighted tension between Sunni and Shi'ite communities (chapter 6) and between nationals and migrant workers (chapter 7). It exposed the weakness of the Gulf states' security forces (chapter 8) and added new burdens to economies already in recession (chapter 9). Finally, it presented the ruling families with a number of challenges to their traditional method of rule (chapter 10).

1. THE THREAT FROM WITHIN

On 23 December 1991 the six GCC rulers gathered in Kuwait for their first summit since the Gulf war. The setting was apt. Only ten months earlier, Kuwait had been liberated from Iraqi occupation by a giant international force led by the United States. The rulers were thankful for Kuwait's rescue, but the mood was sombre. The region as a whole and the GCC states in particular had passed through a terrible ordeal.

The theme of the summit was the defence of the Gulf from future threats. Should the GCC states build up a joint army of their own, as Sultan Qabus of Oman proposed? Should they rely on the 'six plus two' formula – the wartime alliance of the six GCC states plus Egypt and Syria? Or should they acknowledge – in denial of the principle of self-reliance on which the GCC had been founded – that their safety depended, first and foremost, on a Western shield?

That theme is beyond the scope of this report.[2] But while the rulers grappled with issues of external security, there were noises off-stage which suggested that the war had unleashed pressures for internal change.

● A group of Kuwaiti lawyers and academics presented a petition to the summit calling for greater democracy.

● An academic from Bahrain, the Sunni theologian Dr Abdel Latif al-Mahmoud, was arrested after returning home from Kuwait where he had addressed a meeting at the university and criticized the lack of freedom in the GCC states and the concentration of power in the hands of the rulers.[3]

---

[2] For issues of Gulf defence, see Richard Dalton, *Winning Peace in the Gulf: A Long-Term View*, London, Royal Institute of International Affairs, 1992.

[3] Sara el-Gammal, 'Kuwaiti Intellectuals Protest Arrest of Bahraini', Reuters, Kuwait, 17 December 1991. Dr Mahmoud was held for two weeks, then released on bail; a court later cleared him of 'incitement to revolution'.

● In Qatar some 50 members of prominent families presented a petition to the emir, Sheikh Khalifa, calling for an elected assembly and a permanent constitution guaranteeing democracy.[4]

● In Saudi Arabia, the head of the *ulema* (religious scholars), Sheikh Abdel Aziz Bin Baz, warned radical young preachers and intellectuals – members of the kingdom's dominant Wahhabi sect of Sunni Islam – against spreading 'lies and false rumours'. This followed a spate of critical sermons, often circulated on cassette, attacking corruption, Westernization, the kingdom's close relationship with the United States, and its participation in the Middle East peace process.[5]

Taken in isolation, such developments might signify little. Taken together, they suggest an undercurrent of dissent which was a direct product of the war.[6] President Bush and other Western leaders had stressed that this had been a just war against a tyrant who had violated human rights on a massive scale. This, and talk of a 'new world order', had implied to many Arabs that the winds of change – which had toppled communism and the Berlin wall and brought about pressure for democracy in Europe, Africa and Asia – were blowing through the Middle East too.

For the Gulf rulers, however, such pressures posed obvious difficulties. Democracy could be destabilizing, as the example of Algeria showed. But ignoring or suppressing demands for change could also be destabilizing. The war, in short, had highlighted the threat from within as well as the threat from without.

---

[4] 'Qataris Issue Petition for Democracy', AFP, Manama, 18 January 1992.

[5] Bin Baz's remarks can be found in BBC Monitoring, *Summary of World Broadcasts*, Part 4, 30 December 1991.

[6] Youssef Azmeh, 'Undercurrent of Dissent Starts to Surface in Gulf', Reuters, Dubai, 23 January 1992.

4

2. THE RULING FAMILIES

Most of the ruling dynasties of the Gulf trace their roots back more than two centuries. The rise of the Al Saud in Saudi Arabia can be dated from their alliance in the mid-eighteenth century with the Wahhabi religious reform movement. The Al Sabah of Kuwait and the Al Khalifa of Bahrain both have their origins in tribal migrations from central Arabia in the eighteenth century. A unique feature of the Al Khalifa, however, is that they won power by conquest when they drove the Persians from the islands of Bahrain in 1783. The Al bu Said dynasty of Oman was founded in the 1740s. The Al Thani of Qatar, relative newcomers, established their dynasty in the 1860s.[7]

Of the seven ruling families of the United Arab Emirates, the Al Nahyan established themselves in Abu Dhabi during the eighteenth century, and the Al Maktum in Dubai in the 1830s. The Al Qasimi of Sharjah and Ras al-Khaimah trace their origins to the powerful Qawasim tribal grouping of the eighteenth and nineteenth centuries. (The families of the smaller UAE emirates are the Nuayyim of Ajman, the Al Mualla of Umm al-Qaiwain and the Sharqiyyin of Fujairah.)

Two developments have crucially shaped the power and status of the ruling families: the Pax Britannica, and the discovery and exploitation of oil. Between 1820 and Britain's withdrawal from the Gulf in 1971, the Arab sheikhdoms of the Gulf coast were in 'treaty relationship' with Britain. They were not technically colonies or protectorates, but Britain ran their defence and foreign policies, by and large leaving local matters alone. A former British diplomat has remarked that 'until well into the twentieth century nothing was done to release the shaykhdoms from the fragmented isolation in which, as in aspic, the treaties preserved them'.[8]

Britain protected the sheikhdoms from their bigger neighbours, Saudi Arabia, Iraq and Iran, all of which put forward territorial claims at various times. In the 1920s the threat came from the Ikhwan (or Brethren), the holy warriors of Ibn Saud who united most of Arabia and

---

[7] For a succinct introduction to the ruling families and their historical background, see Rosemarie Said Zahlan, *The Making of the Modern Gulf States,* London, Unwin Hyman, 1989.

[8] Glen Balfour-Paul, *The End of Empire in the Middle East*, Cambridge, Cambridge University Press, 1991, p. 103.

became Saudi Arabia's first king in 1932. The fanatical Ikhwan might have conquered the whole of the Arabian peninsula if Britain had not set the limits to Saudi expansion. Later the threat came from Iraq, which claimed Kuwait, and from Iran, which claimed Bahrain. So it is thanks to a century and a half of British dominance in the Gulf that the present ruling families hold power, and it was imperial Britain which drew and protected their frontiers.

Traditionally, a ruler's position depended upon his personal abilities, the support of his family and the backing or at least acquiescence of the leading merchant families. While the ruler often exercised considerable power, the principle of *shura* (consultation) was long established. The ruler had to maintain what has been called a 'balance of oligarchy'.[9]

Oil was discovered at different times (in Bahrain, Kuwait and Saudi Arabia in the 1930s, in Qatar in 1940, in Abu Dhabi and Oman in the 1960s, in Dubai and Sharjah in the 1970s) and in different quantities – at present rates of production, Saudi reserves will last over 80 years, Kuwait's and Abu Dhabi's over 100 years, Oman's little more than a decade and a half.[10]

Oil wealth not only ushered in a period of rapid modernization but strengthened the position of the ruling families. It gave them the means to create the structures of modern states, and to become the dispensers of wealth and welfare. Petrodollars generated waste and corruption; huge sums were spent on lavish lifestyles and on white-elephant projects of many kinds. But at the same time oil revenues gave the rulers great power and patronage. They ensured that the most important and sensitive cabinet posts – defence, the interior, foreign affairs – were kept in the hands of trusted family members. In addition, while giving priority to economic and social development, they took care to maintain at least the outward forms of Muslim piety and to respect the inherent conservatism of their societies.

It was thus as 'newly emergent post-traditional states' (to use Peterson's phrase – see note 9) that the Gulf monarchies faced a series of challenges following Britain's withdrawal from the Gulf in 1971. These included the oil shocks of the 1970s and 1980s, the Iranian revolution, the Afghan conflict, the Iran–Iraq war and, most recently, the Gulf crisis of 1990–91. They survived all these crises with their territorial integrity and their systems of one-family rule intact. Nevertheless, the Gulf crisis posed particular challenges and raised fundamental questions about future stability.

---

[9] J. E. Peterson, *The Arab Gulf States: Steps Toward Political Participation*, New York, Praeger with CSIS, 1988, p. 27. Peterson refers specifically to Kuwait, but the phrase seems applicable more widely.

[10] *BP Statistical Review of World Energy*, London, British Petroleum, June 1992, p. 2.

3. ISLAM AND THE HOUSE OF SAUD

'Saddam did the unthinkable,' King Fahd is reported to have remarked to his ministers on 6 August 1990, four days after Iraq's invasion of Kuwait, 'and therefore we have to do the unthinkable.'[11]

It was 'unthinkable' to invite Western forces into the kingdom because of Saudi Arabia's unique position in the Muslim world as the cradle of Islam and the guardian of Mecca and Medina, the religion's two holiest places. In open acknowledgment of this grave responsibility, since 1986 King Fahd has styled himself 'Servant of the Two Holy Places' – a sign of the crucial role of Islam in lending legitimacy to the House of Saud.

His decision to invite predominantly non-Muslim forces to the Arabian peninsula has been described as without precedent in the 1,300 years since the rise of Islam.[12] One writer has suggested it was rather like a fifteenth-century Pope inviting Ottoman forces to protect the Vatican.[13]

There are differing accounts of the deliberations within the House of Saud prior to the king's decision. The Egyptian writer Mohammed Heikal says Fahd and his brothers were initially reluctant to call for American help, but faced 'open revolt' from younger princes such as Bandar bin Sultan, the ambassador in Washington.[14] Some accounts suggest the king's half-brother, Crown Prince Abdullah, had strong reservations about American intervention.[15]

'Consensus,' as William Quandt has observed, 'is not just a traditional virtue. It is also the key to the Saud family's survival.'[16] Given the enormity of the decision he had to take, Fahd took care to consult both the family and the senior *ulema*. In neither group was there

---

[11] Elaine Sciolino, *The Outlaw State: Saddam Hussein's Quest for Power and the Gulf Crisis*, New York, John Wiley, 1991, p. 220.

[12] Walid Khalidi, *The Middle East Postwar Environment*, Washington, DC, Institute for Palestine Studies, 1991, p. 21.

[13] Philip Robins, 'Engulfed', *London Review of Books*, 30 August 1990.

[14] Mohammed Heikal, *Illusions of Triumph: An Arab View of the Gulf War*, London, Harper Collins, 1992, p. 210.

[15] For example, Bob Woodward, *The Commanders*, New York and London, Simon & Schuster, 1991, p. 271.

[16] William Quandt, *Saudi Arabia in the 1980s*, Washington, DC, Brookings Institution, 1981, p. 83.

unanimity. When called upon to issue a *fatwa* (religious edict) legitimizing the decision, the senior religious scholar, Sheikh Abdel Aziz Bin Baz, used guarded language. In the cause of resisting aggression, he said, it was legitimate to seek the help of Muslims and 'others' – whom he was careful not to specify.[17]

Bin Baz's caution was understandable. The Gulf crisis unleashed a ferment of debate within the kingdom which, more than two years later, has scarcely abated. The crisis led to four developments of particular significance: a climate of openness which brought a breath of fresh air into a closed and conservative society; a backlash from Islamic traditionalists and from a new breed of young Islamic radicals; pressure for change from modernizing liberals; and, finally, the announcement – a year after the end of the war – of long-awaited political reforms.

ARABIAN GLASNOST

The crisis brought Western journalists, as well as Western troops, into the kingdom, and Saudis suddenly found themselves under the intense spotlight of international scrutiny. It was, to put it mildly, a novel experience.

The ruling family found it needed its own media to play a more aggressive role to counter the propaganda emanating from Iraq and its allies. Saddam was denouncing the Gulf sheikhs as un-Islamic, while proclaiming himself, however implausibly, the leader of a jihad against the infidel West. Particularly offensive were his constant attacks questioning the fitness of the House of Saud to guard the Muslim holy places, and his disdainful references to the kingdom, in pre-Saudi terms, as the Hijaz and Nejd.

The Saudi media took up the challenge. Newspapers suddenly became readable. Pan-Arab issues in particular were handled with unheard-of candour. The ruling family encouraged this to happen because, like all the ruling families of the Gulf, it was fighting for its life and had to do so with all the means at its disposal. But the unintended consequence was that ordinary Saudis got a taste of freedom and found they liked it. Tongues were loosened, and the national debate went off in directions Fahd can never have envisaged.[18]

AN ISLAMIC BACKLASH

Many Saudis had misgivings about the arrival of Western forces. Why was their country, which had spent billions of dollars on (mostly Western) arms, so shamefully unable to defend itself? What impact would the influx of Westerners have on the kingdom's way of life? How long would the foreigners stay? And what would they expect in return for their help?

---

[17] James Piscatori, 'Religion and Realpolitik', in James Piscatori (ed.), *Islamic Fundamentalisms and the Gulf Crisis*, Chicago, The Fundamentalism Project, American Academy of Arts and Sciences, 1991, p. 9. Bin Baz, a blind sheikh in his eighties, achieved notoriety in the 1960s when he wrote an essay asserting that the sun goes round the earth. In 1984 he told a student from Kuwait University that women who attended co-educational institutions were no better than prostitutes. 'He also castigated musicians and asserted that it is un-Islamic to photograph any living creature.' *Persian Gulf States: Country Studies*, Washington, DC, The American University, 1985, p. xxi.

[18] For further accounts of the impact of the war on the Saudi kingdom, see Judith Miller, 'The Struggle Within', *New York Times*, 10 March 1991, and Tony Horwitz, 'A Surge of Patriotism Among the Saudis', *Wall Street Journal* (European edition), 15–16 February 1991.

It was not necessary to be a religious zealot to think such thoughts. But a minority went much further, seeing the invitation to Western forces as utterly unforgivable. 'If Iraq has occupied Kuwait,' thundered the radical preacher Dr Safa al-Hawali, 'then America has occupied Saudi Arabia. The real enemy is not Iraq. It is the West.'[19]

The radicals hated Saddam Hussein – indeed they upbraided the Al Saud for backing him against Iran in the 1980s – but they hated America, the Great Satan, even more. Their criticism was all the more dangerous because it came from the heart of Wahhabi Islam. Young men such as Safa al-Hawali and Sheikh Salman al-Owda belong to a new breed of religious radicals. Al-Hawali is dean of Islamic studies at Umm al-Qura University in Mecca. Al-Owda is the dean of the Qasim branch of Imam Muhammad bin Saud University. Both are former students of Bin Baz. Their Islamic credentials are impeccable.

A month after Iraq's invasion of Kuwait, Al-Owda gave a sermon known as 'The Fall of Nations', identifying corruption, nepotism and the absence of free expression as the principal causes of the decay of nation-states. Taped copies of the sermon were seized by the authorities.[20]

These were men of some education. Al-Hawali laced his sermons with quotations from the memoirs of Richard Nixon and the pages of *Foreign Affairs*. Moreover, their list of grievances was by no means confined to issues directly related to the war. Their targets included:

● inequalities of wealth within the kingdom;[21]

● the corruption or incompetence of members of the ruling family;

● the family's tendency to act as if above the law;

● policies of secularization, in education and other fields, which were deemed to dilute Islamic values;

● the payment or charging of interest by banks;

● the kingdom's lack of a strong army;

● a foreign policy which befriended dictators (Assad of Syria, Saddam of Iraq) who repressed their Muslim populations.

Many of the worst fears of the Islamic militants were fulfilled when, in November, three months after Iraq's invasion of Kuwait, a group of between 40 and 50 Saudi women demonstrated in favour of the right to drive. The action of the women, in briefly driving their cars in the capital Riyadh, was quickly picked up by the Western media. (An amateur video of the event was subsequently shown on BBC television.) Within the kingdom, it provoked

---

[19] Mamoun Fandy, 'The Hawali Tapes', *New York Times*, 24 November 1990.

[20] Robert Fisk, 'Subversive Sermons Rock the Cradle of Islam', *The Independent*, 29 November 1990.

[21] 'You see in our societies rich people who own vast palaces and plush cars. Next to this you see a poor man living in a shack. God did not give us this wealth so that we could build palaces.' An extract from a taped sermon quoted (in Arabic) on BBC Television's *Panorama*, 7 January 1991.

a storm of protest from outraged Muslims. The women were denounced and even threatened with death; they and their families were harassed; those who were university teachers lost their jobs.[22]

They had misjudged the moment. At a time of grave national crisis the House of Saud could not afford to upset the *ulema* and the religious conservatives by taking a lenient view of such behaviour. It was the method of protest, as well as the issue, which caused such outrage. Street protest is not the Saudi style.

One of the liberal princes, Talal bin Abdel Aziz, supported the women's right to drive. But the views of senior members of the family were more accurately reflected by Prince Nayef bin Abdel Aziz, the Minister of the Interior, who criticized the demonstration and referred darkly to 'alien influences'. It was Nayef who issued a decree giving the previously informal ban on women drivers the force of law.[23]

Another sign of the Islamic backlash was the sharp increase in the activities of the *mutawa* (religious police). The bearded, cane-wielding *mutawa* ensure that shops and businesses close at prayer times, that no alcohol is sold or consumed, that there is no mingling of the sexes, and that women in public places are covered from head to toe.[24] During the Gulf crisis groups of religious police clashed with Western military personnel, raided homes where parties were under way, and created a climate of fear on the streets and in the shopping centres.

Their targets were Saudis as well as foreigners. In one unusual incident, a Riyadh family went public to demand the punishment of a group of *mutawa* who had forced off the road a car carrying a young Saudi woman, her two maids and her Sudanese driver. They accused her of being immodestly dressed and wearing make-up.[25]

Aware that many liberal Saudis and foreigners alike regarded the *mutawa* as a nuisance and an anachronism, King Fahd, in late 1990, appointed a moderate theologian as their new head. But this had little discernible effect on *mutawa* activity.

LIBERAL LOBBYING

The crisis polarized the debate between Islamic conservatives and modernizing liberals – the mostly Western-educated technocrats, businessmen, academics and others who want to see the adoption of modern laws and a modern system of government and an easing of the Islamic restrictions on everyday life.

The liberals watched aghast when women demonstrators were pilloried and the *mutawa* acted as a law unto themselves. However, towards the end of 1990 and in early 1991, they circulated a petition which was to serve as a catalyst in the new national debate. It was signed

---

[22] For background, see Eleanor Abdella Doumato, 'Women and the Stability of Saudi Arabia', *Middle East Report*, July–August 1991. Bedouin women, in rural areas far from the prying eyes of the *mutawa* (religious police), sometimes drive pick-up trucks, much to the envy of their urban sisters. Marianne Alireza, 'Women of Saudi Arabia', *National Geographic*, October 1987.

[23] The remarks of both princes were reported in *Mideast Mirror*, 16 November 1990.

[24] For background, see Ayman Al-Yassini, *Religion and State in the Kingdom of Saudi Arabia*, Boulder, Colorado, Westview Press, 1985, pp. 68–70.

[25] Jean-Pierre Perrin, 'Saudi Religious Police Crack Down on Moral Offences', AFP, Riyadh, 19 December 1990; Neil MacFarquhar, 'Since Gulf Crisis, Confrontations with Religious Police Rising', AP, Dhahran, 23 December 1990.

by some 40 people, including a former Minister of Information, businessmen from prominent families, and a number of writers and academics. The petition listed ten demands:

1 A flexible approach to the interpretation of the *Sharia* (Islamic law)
2 The issuing of a 'basic law' of government
3 The formation of a consultative council 'representing all regions of the kingdom'
4 The revival of municipal councils
5 Steps to modernize the judicial system and ensure its independence
6 Equality of all citizens 'without distinction based on ethnic, tribal, sectarian, or social origins'
7 Greater freedom for the media
8 Reform of the *mutawa*
9 A greater role for women in public life
10 'Comprehensive and fundamental reform' of the education system.[26]

The petition failed to evoke much response from the ruling family, but it caused a sufficient stir within Saudi society to prompt a group of religious figures to circulate a rival petition. Presented to the king a few months after the war,[27] it was signed by several hundred Islamic scholars and preachers, including senior members of the *ulema*. The petition set out twelve demands:

1 The formation of a consultative council comprising 'honest' and 'totally independent' individuals
2 The conformity of all laws and regulations with the Sharia
3 The need for government officials to be 'unswervingly moral'
4 'Full equality among citizens, not favouring the nobles or begrudging the weak'
5 A purge of government officials of proven 'corruption or dereliction'
6 Fair distribution of public wealth, and the need for banks to be 'cleansed of usury'
7 The creation of a strong and fully integrated army
8 The reform of the media so that they 'serve Islam'
9 The need for foreign alliances to be 'sanctioned by the *Sharia*'
10 The development and strengthening of religious institutions
11 The 'full and effective independence' of judicial institutions

---

[26] The texts of the liberal petition – and of the rival religious petition (see below) – are usefully contained in *Empty Reforms: Saudi Arabia's New Basic Laws*, New York, Middle East Watch, May 1992, pp. 59–62.

[27] Middle East Watch (see note 26, above) gives a date of February 1991 for the 'religious' petition; most sources say it was presented to the king in May.

12 Guarantees – 'within acceptable religious safeguards' – of 'the rights of individuals and of society'.

There is an interesting degree of overlap between the two petitions. Both call for a consultative council, the independence of the judiciary and the equality of all citizens. But this time the king was stung into action. He summoned the senior *ulema* to explain themselves. Shortly afterwards they issued a statement criticizing the way in which the religious petition had been made public – but, significantly, without disowning its demands.[28]

Throughout 1991, the debate continued. Demands and counter-demands were faxed, photocopied and argued over.[29]

In the summer, a group of *ulema* issued a series of clarifications of the religious petition, and complained that some of the signatories had been harassed by the authorities, banned from travelling and called in for interrogation.[30]

By the end of the year, confrontation was in the air. The patience of the ruling family was wearing thin. In the first of a series of warnings, Bin Baz told the militants not to spread 'lies and false rumours'.[31] In an unusual step, Prince Turki bin Faisal, the head of intelligence, spoke out in a mosque in Riyadh, warning the zealots that enough was enough.[32] The king himself issued a warning, albeit in characteristically muted language.[33] A little over a month later, Fahd announced three new laws.

KING FAHD'S REFORMS

Saudi Arabia's first king, Ibn Saud, had promised to issue a 'basic law' of government when the kingdom was created in 1932. The promise had been repeated thirty years later by Crown Prince (later King) Faisal. Fahd himself, first as crown prince and later as king, had on several occasions – for example, after the siege of the Great Mosque in Mecca in 1979[34] – pledged to introduce a basic law, a consultative council and other reforms of the kingdom's system of government.

But nothing had happened – that is, not until 1 March 1992. The striking thing about Fahd's reforms is not their content, which is extremely modest, but the fact that he introduced them at all. It took an earthquake to push Saudi Arabia towards a very cautious, very gradual

---

[28] Piscatori, 'Religion and Realpolitik', p. 10.

[29] 'Fax and opinions', *The Economist*, 15 June 1991.

[30] *Mideast Mirror*, 1 August 1991.

[31] A statement read on Saudi television; see BBC Monitoring, *Summary of World Broadcasts*, 30 December 1991.

[32] Youssef Ibrahim, 'The Saudis Are Fearful, too, as Islam's Militant Tide Rises', *New York Times*, 31 December 1991.

[33] He declared: 'So long as we are able to pursue calm and balanced paths in dealing with certain behaviour, there is no need to resort to other means. However, if a matter transgresses its limit, for every occurrence there is a response.' *Mideast Mirror*, 28 January 1992.

[34] In November 1979 a group of Saudi and other Arab zealots, led by Juhayman al-Otaybi, seized the Great Mosque, denounced the Saudi ruling family and proclaimed the arrival of the Mahdi (redeemer). The fourteen-day siege was ended with much loss of life. On Juhayman's view of the 'tarnished credentials' of the Al Saud, see Joseph Kechichian, 'Islamic Revivalism and Change in Saudi Arabia: Juhayman al-Utaybi's "Letters" to the Saudi People', *The Muslim World*, Vol. LXXX, January 1990, pp. 1–16.

political evolution. The reforms were a response not just to the external drama in the Gulf, but to the pressures of internal dissent and criticism within the kingdom itself.

The king put forward, first, a basic law of government.[35] The 83 articles of the basic law proclaim the Islamic character of the state, the sanctity of family values, the powers of the king and the Council of Ministers, the rights and duties of the citizen, the economic principles of the kingdom, and mechanisms of government accountability.

Several points are noteworthy. The rules of succession (article 5) acknowledge, for the first time, that power will eventually pass from the sons to the grandsons of Ibn Saud. The law proclaims the sanctity of both public money (article 16) and private property (article 18). Article 26 declares that: 'The state guarantees human rights in accordance with the Islamic Sharia.' The state has a duty to provide job opportunities (article 28), education and literacy (article 30), health care (article 31), protection of the environment (article 32) and security for all citizens and residents (article 36). Article 37 states, in an implicit curb on the activities of the *mutawa*: 'The home is sacrosanct and shall not be entered without the permission of the owner or be searched except in cases specified by law.' The information media are instructed to be courteous and not to harm 'the state's security and its public relations' (article 39). The judiciary is proclaimed to be independent (article 46).

The second law creates a 60-member *majlis al-shura* (consultative council). The members, 'chosen by the king from among scholars and men of knowledge and expertise' (article 3), will be able to propose laws but not pass them. They will advise the king and his ministers on domestic issues, and will also be able to 'study international laws, charters, treaties and agreements, and concessions' (article 15). The council will be based in Riyadh (article 12) and sit for four years (article 13).

The third law gives the country's regions a measure of autonomy. Each region is to have an emir, who is to be accountable to the Minister of the Interior (articles 4–5), and an advisory council, chaired by the emir and containing not less than ten suitably qualified members of the public (article 16).

A respected human rights group has described the king's new laws as 'empty reforms'.[36] In a well-documented 62-page report it points out – as have Saudi oppositionists – that rather than introducing significant change, the laws essentially formalize the status quo. (Indeed the king himself gives this impression in the preamble to the new laws. 'These three statutes', he declares, 'are to strengthen something that exists and to formulate something which is already in operation.') In addition, the reforms do little to protect human rights, ensure fair trials, or improve conditions for foreign workers or the kingdom's Shi'ite minority.

The king himself, in an interview with a Kuwaiti newspaper, underlined the strict limits of political change in Saudi Arabia. 'The prevailing democratic system in the world is not suitable for us in this region,' he declared. 'Elections do not fall within the sphere of the Muslim religion.'[37]

---

[35] For the full texts of the laws, see BBC Monitoring, *Summary of World Broadcasts*, 3–4 March 1992.

[36] Middle East Watch (see note 26, above); For other critical assessments, see the interview with Tawfiq al-Shaikh, a Shi'ite oppositionist, in *The Independent*, 3 March 1992, and *Mideast Mirror* of the same date.

[37] Interview with *Al-Siyasah*, 28 March 1992; English translation in BBC Monitoring, Summary of World Broadcasts, 30 March 1992.

Nevertheless, the package of reforms, for all its limitations, reinforced the sense that change was in the air, and that the House of Saud was having to adjust, willingly or unwillingly, to new realities.[38]

IMPLICATIONS

Three conclusions may be drawn from these developments. First, the Saudi rulers have cut a stick to beat their own backs. The Islamic institutions they have built up over the years have served to nurture a new generation of Islamic militants, some of whom are now vigorously critical of the ruling family, its policies and its lifestyle. In an essay published just before the Gulf war, an American expert accurately predicted the danger:

> The kingdom is particularly vulnerable to religiously motivated criticism and its Islamic institutions (such as the Islamic universities and organs of international proselytizing) may serve also as channels of organization for disenchanted elements within the country and for alliances with similar movements outside.[39]

In this respect, the risks the kingdom has run in its domestic policy mirror those it has encountered in its foreign policy. Saudi Arabia has consistently supported a wide range of Muslim groups and institutions throughout the world in the hope that they would share its moderate and pro-Western orientation. This hope has not always been well founded, as its experience in the Gulf war illustrated.[40]

Second, it is hard to see how the *ulema*, divided and disgruntled, can continue to provide the legitimizing role for which they have been groomed. The *ulema* are unhappy at the king's reforms, seeing them as a means of diluting their influence. After several months of silence following the announcement of the reforms, a 'memorandum' started to circulate, apparently signed by about 100 religious figures. The document called for changes including a bigger role for the *ulema* in decision-making, less government control of mosques, the scrapping of laws inconsistent with the *Sharia* and greater help for the urban and rural poor.[41]

Third, the old balancing act played by the Al Saud has become more difficult to perform. Hitherto it has sought to position itself between the Islamic conservatives and the modernizing liberals, sometimes deferring to the one, sometimes to the other. But Islamic dissent has become harder to handle. On many issues[42] the religious conservatives can

---

[38] Alain Gresh, 'Les nouveaux visages de la contestation islamique en Arabie saoudite', *Le Monde Diplomatique*, August 1992.

[39] J. E. Peterson, 'Change and Continuity in Arab Gulf Society', in Charles Davies (ed.), *After the War: Iraq, Iran and the Arab Gulf*, Chichester, Carden Publications, 1990.

[40] See 'Militant Islam's Saudi Paymasters', *Guardian*, 29 February 1992; and for an account of how Islamic movements responded to the Gulf war, Piscatori, *Islamic Fundamentalisms and the Gulf Crisis*.

[41] See the Paris-based newsletter *Issues*, September 1992, pp. 2–3. On 17 September, in an angry denunciation of the 'memorandum', the senior *ulema* denied that it had Bin Baz's backing.

[42] But not all; a conservative campaign against *riba* (interest) failed to deter private investors when one of the kingdom's biggest banks launched a share flotation in January 1992. Sandy Feustel, 'Cash-rich Saudis Snap up Shares in Market Boom', AP, Riyadh, 25 February 1992.

probably count on a good deal of popular support. Most Saudis are probably against women driving cars; most are probably unhappy at the idea of having normal relations with Israel; most are against corruption and profligacy. The triangular balance of power between conservatives, liberals and the Al Saud family is changing, with consequences which are not easy to predict.

This new balance of power could affect the question of succession, since the *ulema* and the Islamic opposition appear to prefer Crown Prince Abdullah to Fahd. Abdullah's efforts to maintain his Arab and Islamic connections, and to distance himself from the United States, may therefore stand him in good stead. However, any significant shift in Saudi Arabia's orientation would provoke opposition from, among others, the younger, pro-American princes such as the ambitious and capable Bandar.[43]

A new external crisis, triggered from Baghdad or elsewhere, might bring these simmering issues to a head. By itself, domestic discontent may be containable; coupled with wider regional problems, it could pose a more formidable challenge.

---

[43] 'A flashy, handsome man-about-town...activist, charming, profane. The former air force pilot was a kind of Arab Gatsby. ...' Bob Woodward, *Veil: The Secret Wars of the CIA*, New York, Simon & Schuster, 1987, p. 351. For Bandar's ambitions to the throne, see Peter Theroux, 'Letter from Riyadh', *Vanity Fair*, April 1991.

4. RIPPLES IN THE LOWER GULF

How far have such pressures for change, both during and after the war, been apparent in other GCC states?

BAHRAIN

A few months after Iraq's invasion of Kuwait, Bahrain's Prime Minister, Sheikh Khalifa bin Salman Al Khalifa, expressed support for the reintroduction of democracy[44] – absent since 1975, when the emirate's short-lived experiment with an elected parliament was terminated. In August 1991, he again indicated that reforms were on the way, and that freedom of opinion and expression would be guaranteed.

There are two Bahrains: the islands of calm and stability beloved by expatriate businessmen, and the controlled, repressive state depicted by Bahraini exiles and in the pages of human rights reports.[45] Bahrain is the only GCC state with a Shi'ite majority. Many of the country's Shi'ites are comfortably off, but there are simmering economic grievances – including high unemployment – among the less privileged.[46]

Sectarian politics, and the ruling family's reluctance to share power, led to the dissolution of the elected 30-member assembly which functioned between 1973 and 1975. Since then, the emirate has had no assembly, either elected or appointed.

Following the Khomeini revolution of 1979, Iran revived its claim to Bahrain as its fourteenth province (just as Iraq was later to claim Kuwait as its nineteenth province). In December 1981 the authorities in Bahrain announced the discovery of an Iranian-backed plot to attack government buildings and high-ranking officials and set up an Islamic republic. More than 70 people, said to belong to the Islamic Front for the Liberation of Bahrain, were brought to trial and given prison sentences ranging from seven years to life.[47]

---

[44] *Gulf Daily News*, 12 December 1990.

[45] See, for example, *Bahrain: Time for Change*, a sixteen-page report by the human rights group Article 19, London, December 1991.

[46] Overall unemployment may be as high as 20 per cent; see *Financial Times*, Bahrain Survey, 14 July 1992.

[47] Fred Lawson, *Bahrain: The Modernization of Autocracy*, Boulder, Colorado, Westview Press, 1989, pp. 86–87; Joseph Kostiner, 'Shi'i Unrest in the Gulf', in Martin Kramer (ed.), *Shi'ism, Resistance, and Revolution*, Boulder, Colorado, Westview Press, 1987, p. 180.

Since then, and especially since the Gulf crisis of 1990–91, relations with Iran have improved – and Shi'ite oppositionists have tended to moderate their demands, advocating constitutional democracy rather than the violent overthrow of the government.

However, Bahrain has remained politically frozen. The emir, Sheikh Isa, in power for more than 30 years, appears to share the view of his father, Sheikh Salman, who told the British Political Resident in 1954: 'It is the function of Government to govern, of the merchants to trade, of the farmers to farm and of the workers to work, and the less any of these groups interfere in the concerns of the other the better.'[48]

But if Saudi Arabia's consultative council comes into being, Bahrain will be the only GCC state without some sort of assembly, and it too may feel under greater pressure to change. Indeed, in the summer of 1992, unofficial reports began to circulate that Bahrain would have a 30-seat consultative council before the end of the year. Some Bahrainis were disappointed, however, at the suggestion that the council would be selected rather than elected.[49]

QATAR

It was a sign of the times that even in tiny, conservative Qatar – often seen as the quietest of the GCC states – a petition calling for fundamental political reform was presented to the emir, Sheikh Khalifa, in December 1991. Signed by some 50 members of prominent families, it criticized government policy on a wide range of issues including education, health, the media, the economy and civil service recruitment, and made two significant demands, for an elected assembly with legislative powers and a permanent constitution guaranteeing democracy. (The country's provisional constitution of 1970, amended in 1972, remains in force.)[50]

The petition received no publicity within Qatar, and very little outside. But it stirred up comment and upset the ruling family, the Al Thani. The signatories, mostly young liberals, were called upon to make a written apology to the emir. When they failed to do so, two were detained for short periods and three were prevented from travelling to a conference in Kuwait.[51]

The petition does not appear, however, to have had an impact on the emirate's political future or on the Al Thani's hold on power.

Qatar has had an advisory council since 1972, when the present emir took power from his cousin. It initially had 20 members and was later expanded to 30. The government generally respects its views but is not bound by them. The emir summoned the council before

---

[48] Quoted by Zahlan, in *The Making of the Modern Gulf States*, p. 56. Chapter 4 of her book provides a concise account of the political evolution of Bahrain. For further background about Bahrain's national assembly, see Peterson, *The Arab Gulf States: Steps Toward Political Participation*, Chapter 3.

[49] 'Bahrain Plans Consultative Assembly', Reuters, Manama, 29 September 1992. One Bahraini quoted to me the Arabic saying: 'After fasting, we ate an onion'; interview in Manama, September 1992.

[50] 'Qataris Issue Petition for Democracy', AFP, Manama, 18 January 1992. The Arabic text of the petition was published in the Gulf opposition magazine *Al-Jazeera al-Arabia*, February 1992.

[51] 'Activists Say Qatar Harassing Petitioners', Reuters, Kuwait, 9 May 1992.

joining Saudi Arabia in inviting Western forces into the region – a sign that the ruling family wished to share the burden of taking such a crucial decision.[52]

UNITED ARAB EMIRATES

No comparable developments occurred in the UAE, and many observers believed that the federation emerged from the Gulf war politically unscathed.[53]

Nevertheless, reformists felt that the crisis showed up the country's fragility and the deficiencies of both local and federal institutions. As elsewhere, there was a sense of local patriotism among nationals; but there were also mixed feelings about Western intervention in the region.

Like all the states of the lower Gulf, the UAE has an advisory assembly, the Federal National Council (FNC), set up in 1972 with 40 members. The biggest emirates, Abu Dhabi and Dubai, have eight seats each; Sharjah and Ras al-Khaimah six each; and the three smallest emirates (Ajman, Umm al-Qaiwain, Fujairah) four each. The members are chosen by the seven rulers, and most are from the business community. All legislation is referred to the council, which has on occasion proved outspoken, especially on economic issues. Abu Dhabi has its own 50-member consultative council which reviews most legislation and has a largely tribal membership.[54] In the UAE, as elsewhere in the lower Gulf, these advisory councils are, however, modest institutions with a limited capacity to act as channels for demands and grievances.

In the UAE, pressure for change has traditionally come from Dubai and Sharjah rather than the more conservative emirate of Abu Dhabi. The earliest movement for political reform was in Dubai in 1938, when members of the ruler's family forced him to accept an elected fifteen-member council. It survived for a mere six months, but the ideas it generated – for curbs on the power of the ruler and for planned economic and social development – have had a more lasting effect.[55]

Pressure for change has often coincided with regional crisis. This happened in 1979, at the time of Iran's revolution, when the FNC issued a memorandum calling for the abolition of the individual emirates and the creation of genuine parliamentary democracy. The memorandum declared that 'economic and social justice is a pillar of internal stability'. The response of Sheikh Rashed, then ruler of Dubai, was revealing: 'A unitary state means no borders, therefore no rulers.'[56]

The reform movements of 1938 and 1979 both fizzled out, but reformist ideas still find expression, particularly in the Sharjah newspaper *Al-Khaleej*. Both during and after the Gulf crisis, *Al-Khaleej* provided a forum in which writers from the UAE and other GCC states could express dissident views. In August 1992 the newspaper organized a symposium at which Gulf intellectuals called for the strengthening of the GCC's institutions, progress

---

[52] For details of the advisory council, see Peterson, *The Arab Gulf States: Steps Toward Political Participation*, pp. 84–91.

[53] 'In contrast to the other GCC states, the UAE authorities at the federal and emirate level have registered no need to even whisper of political reform.' Special report on the UAE, *Middle East Economic Digest*, 1 May 1992.

[54] Peterson, *The Arab Gulf States*, pp. 91–102.

[55] Peterson, *The Arab Gulf States*, pp. 93–95, and Zahlan, *The Making of the Modern Gulf States*, p. 68.

[56] *The Middle East*, June 1980, pp. 29–33.

towards democracy and freedom of expression, and oil policies less tailored to Western interests.[57]

OMAN

Recent political change in Oman has come from above rather than from the grass roots. Always the odd man out in the GCC, the sultanate – although still a conservative and paternalistic state[58] – is held up as something of a model by reformists elsewhere in the region. In comparison with, say, the rulers of Bahrain and Qatar, Sultan Qabus has been politically innovative. In 1981 he set up the country's first representative body, the State Consultative Council (SCC), with an initial membership of 43, later expanded to 55. Its mandate was restricted to bread-and-butter economic and social issues, and it met only three times a year.[59]

During the Gulf crisis, the sultan pledged to advance the process of political participation, and in November 1991 he announced the creation of a new 59-member consultative council (*majlis al-shura*) to replace the SCC. The new council is both bigger and somewhat more representative than its predecessor. (Members are proposed at local level, nominated by regional govenors and finally approved by the sultan.[60])

In the past, only the formal openings of SCC sessions were televised. More recently, Omani viewers have had the novel experience of watching government ministers being grilled by the consultative council on live television. The Information Minister, for example, has been criticized for the poor quality of the official media.[61]

Is Oman pointing the way for other GCC states? Reformists elsewhere argue, 'Even Oman is moving ahead faster than we are.' But it has arguably been easier for Sultan Qabus to embark on political experimentation, albeit cautiously, precisely because Oman is different from its neighbours. With its small population and modest oil wealth, it has been spared much of the social and economic dislocation experienced by its Gulf neighbours. It remains, in many respects, a traditional tribal society, where pressures for change are less marked than in the more frenetic states to the north.[62]

---

[57] *Al-Khaleej*, 5 August 1992, reported in *Mideast Mirror* of the same date.

[58] Tony Horwitz, 'Surface Appearances Matter Very Deeply to a Sultan of Clean', *Wall Street Journal* (European edition), 25 April 1991.

[59] Peterson, *The Arab Gulf States*, pp. 102–108.

[60] *Financial Times*, Survey of Oman, 20 November 1991.

[61] *Mideast Mirror*, 2 June 1992, quoting the approving comments of the editor of a Bahraini weekly.

[62] See the most recent study of Oman under Sultan Qabus, Ian Skeet's *Oman: Politics and Development*, Basingstoke, Macmillan, 1992.

5. KUWAIT: AT WAR WITH ITSELF

In all the GCC states, the Gulf crisis generated expectations which were not fulfilled. But nowhere was the expectation greater, or the disappointment keener, than in Kuwait.

The best that can be said – and hindsight should not blur the achievement – is that the emirate survived. The idea of Kuwait, not just its physical shell, remained intact. Saddam had sought to destroy both. With his limited grasp of liberal democracy, he may well have reckoned that Kuwait's ruling family, the Al Sabah, was so unpopular that its critics could be induced or coerced into accepting Iraqi rule. But the Iraqis searched in vain for Kuwaiti quislings. Even the fiercest critics of the Al Sabah preferred their own imperfect democracy to the tyranny of the Baath.[63]

Kuwait has three things which the other GCC states lack: a parliamentary tradition, organized opposition groups and a relatively free press. Most Kuwaitis are proud of these distinguishing features, and want to keep them. The seven main opposition groups are very diverse, including liberals and leftists, Kuwaiti nationalists and Arab nationalists, and groups representing the Sunni majority and the Shi'ite minority (some 30 per cent of all nationals). Since independence from Britain in 1961, and the proclamation of a democratic constitution the following year, these groups have competed with pro-government forces for representation in a 50-seat parliament.

The franchise is restricted to Kuwaiti males over 21 who can trace their lineage back to 1920 or beyond. Neither women nor the great majority of immigrants can vote.[64]

Twice, in 1976 and again in 1986, the emir has dissolved parliament after it challenged the policies and probity of ministers belonging to the ruling family. On the second occasion, some of the constitution's provisions were suspended.

After the Iraqi invasion, Kuwaiti oppositionists in exile were united in demanding that the parliament and the constitution should be restored once Kuwait was free. And this, in

---

[63] The sentiment was not confined to Kuwait. 'Better the thief than the murderer,' one Dubai oppositionist remarked to me. Interview, May 1992.

[64] Political parties as such are banned. For an account of how Kuwait's clubs and cultural associations have nevertheless evolved into embryonic political parties, see Shafeeq Ghabra, 'Voluntary Associations in Kuwait: The Foundation of a New System?', *Middle East Journal*, Vol. 45, No. 2, Spring 1991.

essence, was what the emir, Sheikh Jaber, and the Crown Prince, Sheikh Saad, promised at a congress they convened in Jiddah two months after the invasion, to which some 1,300 Kuwaitis were invited. They also hinted that women would get the vote.[65]

Planning for the future was not confined to the political sphere. Kuwaitis were conscious that the world's gaze was on them. 'What is Kuwait?' asked *Time* magazine on the cover of its Christmas 1990 edition, adding the tart rider: 'And is it worth dying for?' Uncomfortably aware of the West's cynicism about waging war to make the Gulf 'safe for feudalism', many Kuwaitis discovered the virtues of self-reliance. In the emirate itself, they collected rubbish, baked bread, did the housework – jobs previously done by foreigners. In exile, others drew up the blueprint for a brave new postwar Kuwait which would be fully democratic, based on merit and accountability, and no longer dependent on armies of Arab and Asian migrant workers. This idea was by no means simply the propaganda of the Al Sabah, though the ruling family did nothing to discourage it. Many Kuwaitis seemed genuinely imbued with a new spirit of pride and patriotism.

It was not to last. The new Kuwait has not materialized. Instead, after the expulsion of Iraqi troops in February 1991, the country has in many ways been at war with itself.

SETTLING OF SCORES

The aftermath of liberation saw a brutal settling of scores. In three months of anarchy, armed gangs wreaked vengeance on Palestinians, Sudanese, Yemenis and others accused of collaborating with the Iraqi occupiers. Some 300,000 Palestinians were either hounded out or denied permission to return; by the summer of 1992 only 20,000–25,000 remained. Flagrant human rights abuses occurred. Opposition figures alleged that young members of the ruling family had set up militias which were roaming the streets intimidating not only Palestinians but also pro-democracy activists.[66]

Before the war, there had been three faultlines in Kuwaiti society: between government and opposition, between nationals and non-nationals, and between Sunni and Shi'ite. The war added a fourth: between those who stayed and those who left. Some of those who had spent the war in comfortable exile sought to compensate for their absence by bullying alleged collaborators.

The need for law and order was one of the most urgent problems facing the postwar government, but there were plenty of others. Opposition groups felt the promises made in Jiddah had been broken, and indeed they were at best fulfilled in reluctant and dilatory fashion. The opposition disliked the imposition of martial law for the first four months after liberation; they chafed at press censorship; they opposed as unconstitutional the decision to maintain, as an interim assembly, the rather toothless advisory council, a partly elected, partly appointed body introduced before the war. And when, in April, the emir announced parliamentary elections, opposition groups were dismayed that voting would not be until

[65] Milton Viorst, 'After the Liberation', *New Yorker*, 30 September 1991.

[66] Milton Viorst, 'After the Liberation'; 'Murder, torture, arbitrary detention and unlawful deportation have been the tools of this campaign of vengeance', declared the human rights group Middle East Watch in introducing its 63-page report *A Victory Turned Sour: Human Rights in Kuwait Since Liberation*, New York, September 1991. In addition, see the section on Kuwait in *Country Reports on Human Rights Practices for 1991*, Washington, DC, Department of State, February 1992.

October 1992. They were convinced that by then the Al Sabah would already have taken the key decisions about the country's future.

There were other grievances. Despite the hint made at the Jiddah congress, women were not, after all, to vote in the October elections. (The government argued that constitutionally this was a change only parliament could make.) Moreover, there were plenty of signs that the ruling family was resorting to time-honoured methods of boosting its support in the run-up to the poll. Citizens were wooed with cash handouts. Bad debts worth $20 billion were bought from banks by the government. (This was said to be the emir's idea.) Civil servants' salaries were raised by a quarter. The Al Sabah had, in short, returned to their old autocratic and free-spending ways.

Despite the government's stated aim of making Kuwaitis a majority in their own country, the old dependence on immigrants quickly reasserted itself. Moreover, there was little sign that the Kuwaitis' suffering at the hands of the Iraqis had made them any less inclined to ill treat their foreign workers.[67]

Fear of a resurgent Iraq remained a dominant concern. In September 1991 Kuwait signed a ten-year defence agreement with the United States. Similar agreements were later signed with Britain and France.

On 5 October 1992 Kuwaiti voters turned out in force to elect an independent-minded parliament in which opposition figures held more than 30 of the 50 seats. It was in effect a vote of no confidence in the postwar government led by Crown Prince Sheikh Saad, who in response introduced a new and more broadly based government. But the risk of confrontation, as in 1986, between the parliament and the ruling family remained considerable.

As the only GCC member with an elected parliament, Kuwait will remain a pole of attraction for reformists in neighbouring states. Stability – or instability – in Kuwait therefore has regional ramifications.

---

[67] Chris Hedges, 'Horror Stories from Foreign Labourers in Kuwait, *Herald Tribune*, 7 January 1992; *The Economist*, 22 February 1992; and *Punishing the Victim: Rape and Mistreatment of Asian Maids in Kuwait*, New York, Middle East Watch, August 1992.

6. THE SHI'ITE FACTOR

What impact did the war have on relations between the Sunni and Shi'ite communities of the Gulf?

Table 1 Shi'ites in the GCC states (1984 estimates)

	Shi'ite population	Shi'ites as % of nationals
Saudi Arabia	440,000	8
Bahrain	168,000	70
Kuwait	137,000	24
UAE	45,000	18
Oman	28,000	4
Qatar	11,000	16

Source: Estimates in James Bill, 'Resurgent Islam in the Persian Gulf', *Foreign Affairs*, Fall 1984. The percentage for Bahrain may be a little high, that for Kuwait a little low.

From the late 1970s and throughout the 1980s, a series of worrying developments – the Islamic revolution in Shi'ite Iran, the Iran-Iraq war and Shi'ite subversion in Bahrain and Kuwait – put the Shi'ites of the Arab Gulf under a cloud of suspicion. In two respects the Gulf crisis of 1990–91 helped to lift this cloud. First, Shi'ites showed as much patriotism as Sunnis in the confrontation with Iraq. Indeed they had particular cause to hate Saddam because of his brutal repression of their co-religionists, who form just over half of Iraq's population. Second, the war led to a rapprochement between the GCC states and Iran, causing fear of Iranian-sponsored subversion to recede.

But Shi'ite grievances have not gone away.

The problem is in part sectarian, particularly in Saudi Arabia where many Wahhabi Muslims refuse to regard Shi'ites as true believers. A few months after the end of the war, one of the senior Saudi *ulema*, Sheikh Abdullah bin Jibreen, issued a *fatwa* which denounced

Shi'ites as heretics worthy of death.[68] This was picked up by the press in Iran, and the ensuing fuss strained Saudi–Iranian relations.

Not surprisingly, the Shi'ites of Saudi Arabia's oil-rich Eastern Province see the new Sunni militancy in the kingdom as particularly threatening to themselves.

In part the problem is one of human rights. In Saudi Arabia and Bahrain in particular, any sign of Shi'ite activism is harshly repressed. Amnesty International and other human rights groups report that most human rights abuses in these two countries involve Shi'ites.[69]

Finally, Shi'ites in all GCC states suffer various forms of discrimination. They are often barred from military service and from senior government appointments. Saudi Arabia's national oil company, Saudi Aramco, once known for a recruitment policy which favoured the Shi'ites, began in the 1980s to weed out Shi'ites from responsible positions.[70]

In Bahrain, according to the American State Department,

> Sunnis generally receive preference for employment in sensitive positions, including in the Bahraini Defense Force and managerial ranks in the public sector. Shi'a tend to be employed in lower paid, lesser skilled jobs. Social and municipal services in most Shi'a neighbourhoods, particularly in rural villages, are inferior to those found in Sunni urban communities.[71]

The situation of Shi'ites in the Gulf remains susceptible to external influences. Operation Southern Watch, the Western effort to protect the Shi'ites of southern Iraq which began in the summer of 1992, had an inevitable impact on Shi'ite communities in the GCC states. One reason for Bahrain's nervousness about the operation, for example, was the fact that Shi'ites form a majority of its own population. The death of a leading Shi'ite figure, Ayatollah Khoi, in Iraq in August 1992 prompted demonstrations of public mourning in Bahrain and showed how closely Bahraini Shi'ites follow the fortunes of their co-religionists in neighbouring states.

The changing pattern of relations between Iran and the GCC states will also affect the domestic position of Shi'ite communities. Those relations have been damaged by Iran's effective assertion of sovereignty over Abu Musa, the island at the lower end of the Gulf which has been under the joint control of Iran and the UAE since 1971. This has revived fears that Iran wants a position of hegemony in the Gulf. Regional instability of this kind will tend to hinder the development of stable relations between the Sunni and Shi'ite communities of the GCC states, and perhaps slow the growth of a national consciousness transcending sectarian differences.

---

[68] *Issues*, January 1992; *Empty Reforms*, p. 38.

[69] See, for example, *Amnesty International Report 1992*, London, 1992.

[70] *Country Reports on Human Rights Practices for 1991*, p. 1587.

[71] ibid., p. 1349.

7. MIGRANT WORKERS' MISERY

According to the most recent estimates, immigrants comprise a startling 40 per cent of the total GCC population – over seven million people out of a total of 17.6 million – and over 70 per cent of the workforce.

Table 2 Estimates of the GCC populations (1992)

	Nationals	Non-nationals	Non-nationals as % of total	Total
Bahrain	330,000	134,000	29	464,000
Kuwait	387,000	803,000	67	1,190,000
Oman	1,062,000	380,000	26	1,442,000
Qatar	141,000	272,000	66	413,000
Saudi Arabia	8,066,400	4,192,600	34	12,259,000
UAE	531,000	1,294,000	70	1,825,000
Total	10,500,000	7,100,000	40	17,600,000

Source: Birks Sinclair & Associates, *GCC Market Report 1992*, Durham, 1992.

The Gulf war highlighted the economic, cultural and political problems caused by this high level of dependence on foreign workers. In economic terms, the GCC states are failing to make full use of their own educated people. The national populations of these states are growing rapidly – at between 3 and 4 per cent a year – and, as more and more educated people enter the employment market, there is bound to be increasing competition for jobs between nationals and non-nationals. Moreover, since more women than men are studying at many Gulf universities, there will be growing pressure to open up employment opportunities for women – which in turn will sharpen the conflict between modernizing liberals and religious conservatives.[72]

Second, the presence of immigrants of more than a hundred nationalities has caused a clash of cultures. Gulf families rely on Asian nannies, then complain that their children are learning Urdu or Sinhalese. In 1991 foreigners in the UAE were blamed for 80 per cent of crime (Asians for 60 per cent).[73] A few years earlier, officials in the Emirates discovered that three-quarters of divorces involved cases where a UAE man had married an Asian woman.[74] (Several GCC states restrict marriage between nationals and non-nationals. Omanis are barred from marrying non-Omanis by a decree which has caused some resentment.[75])

Third, citizenship has been denied to all but a handful of foreign workers, even though many have spent a lifetime working in the Gulf. Some Gulf Arabs argue that it would be enlightened self-interest to extend citizenship, thereby giving immigrants a stronger stake in society and bolstering the national demographic base. Others – and this is the dominant view – fear cultural domination and worry that immigrants granted citizenship would start pressing for political rights.

The Gulf crisis highlighted and exacerbated these problems. It is a grim statistic that between five and six million people were uprooted.[76] Among these were the Kurdish and Shi'ite refugees of Iraq. But at least half were Asian workers who fled from Iraq and Kuwait, and expatriate Arabs who were punished for their alleged sympathy for Iraq: these included 800,000 Yemenis forced out of Saudi Arabia and 300,000 Palestinians expelled from Kuwait. What has been called the 'de-Arabization' of the Gulf was under way well before the Gulf crisis.[77] But the crisis gave the process new momentum and a new rationale; this time its purpose was plainly political.

The expulsions were both unwarranted and short-sighted. Individual Palestinians, Yemenis and others may have sympathized and even collaborated with Iraq. But nothing done by individuals or by their political leaders can justify collective punishment inflicted on whole communities. Many of those expelled were ill treated and lost homes, livelihoods and life's savings.

In expelling these groups the GCC states drove still deeper the wedge of mistrust between their national and non-national communities, soured their relations with much of the Arab world, and deprived themselves of skilled workers they could not easily replace.

Migrant workers have strong incentives to keep there heads down. To complain at the denial of the most basic rights is to risk summary deportation. There have been no reports of serious strikes or labour unrest in recent years. But it may be a mistake to assume that because they can earn much more in the Gulf than at home, immigrants will put up with any

---

[72] Peterson, 'The Political Status of Women in the Arab Gulf States', *Middle East Journal*, Vol. 43, No. 1, Winter 1989.

[73] Nadim Kawash, 'In UAE, Oil is Boon and Bane', AFP, Abu Dhabi, 10 July 1992.

[74] Christine Hauser, 'Government Loans Help Keep Romance at Home', Reuters, Abu Dhabi, 15 June 1992.

[75] Ian Skeet, *Oman: Politics and Development,* p. 180, note 170. The rule was introduced in 1986.

[76] Nicholas Van Hear, 'Forced Migration and the Gulf Conflict, 1990-91', *Oxford International Review*, Vol. III, No. 1, Winter 1991; and the same author's update to Roger Owen, *Migrant Workers in the Gulf,* London, Minority Rights Group, 1985.

[77] J. S. Birks, 'The Demographic Challenge in the Arab Gulf', in B. R. Pridham (ed.), *The Arab Gulf and the Arab World*, London, Croom Helm, 1988. The proportion of Arabs in the immigrant workforce fell from over 75 per cent in 1970 to just over half in the late 1980s and under 40 per cent by 1992.

indignity. In some of the GCC states – postwar Kuwait is the most obvious example – the pattern of mistreatment of foreign workers is so persistent that it is creating a simmering resentment which may eventually find expression. Even if it causes no overt political effects it may contribute to an underlying social malaise.

8. DEALING WITH DISSENT

The Gulf war exposed the inadequacy of the GCC states' security forces. As we have seen, critics of Saudi Arabia's ruling family asked pointedly why the kingdom did not have a strong and integrated army. The reason, as they well knew, was the family's deep-seated fear of a military coup, which has led it to maintain two forces: a 73,000-strong army responsible for external security, under the Defence Minister, Prince Sultan; and the National Guard, with 55,000 regulars and 20,000 irregulars, responsible for internal security, under Crown Prince Abdullah.[78]

The National Guard's handling of two serious crises – the capture of the Great Mosque in Mecca in 1979, and riots led by Iranian demonstrators during the Hajj (pilgrimage to Mecca and other holy sites) in 1987 – left it with a reputation for heavy-handedness. Moreover, both incidents showed that there are problems of coordination between the National Guard, the Ministry of Defence and the Ministry of the Interior (which is in charge of the police, the secret police and paramilitary forces).

The Gulf crisis prompted King Fahd to announce plans for the expansion of the security forces (including the National Guard) and even for military conscription. After the war, Saudi officials, seeking to coordinate future security arrangements with the Pentagon, talked of doubling the armed forces to about 200,000 men within the next five to seven years.[79]

Other GCC states have announced similar intentions. But all suffer from the same manpower constraints in the military sector as they do in the civilian sector. Most of Kuwait's soldiers and policemen are non-Kuwaiti. Before the war they included large numbers of *bidoun*, stateless Arabs who have been denied Kuwaiti citizenship. The *bidoun* are thought to number between 150,000 and 200,000; some have lived in Kuwait for several generations. Though some died fighting the Iraqis, many fled and have been denied the right to return. It

---

[78] Figures from *The Military Balance 1992-1993,* London, International Institute for Strategic Studies, 1992, pp. 120–1.

[79] Youssef Ibrahim, 'Saudis Firm on Pentagon Ties', *Herald Tribune*, 26–7 October 1991.

is not clear who will take their place in the army and the police.[80] Indeed the authorities may be forced to resume recruitment of *bidoun* for lack of other options.

After the war, Kuwait announced plans to spend $9 billion on defence. But a conscription drive in 1991 reportedly gained only 2,000 new recruits. Significant expansion of the prewar army of 20,000 looks unrealistic.[81]

The conflict led the UAE – with a prewar army of 44,000 – to begin recruiting women as well as men into its armed forces, a significant change of policy for a conservative Muslim state.[82]

But most GCC states continue to rely on mercenaries from a number of Arab, Asian and Western countries for their defence and internal security. This seems likely to continue for the foreseeable future.[83]

THE ROLE OF THE GCC

Since the creation of the GCC more than a decade ago, internal security has had a collective dimension. The GCC came into being, after all, as a result of external threats with direct implications for internal security. As one writer has put it, 'The Iranian revolution was the catalyst, and the Iran–Iraq war the excuse, which caused the six conservative Gulf monarchies to set up a regional security organization in 1981.'[84]

In 1982 Saudi Arabia signed bilateral security agreements with all the GCC states except Kuwait. Kuwaiti touchiness about anything which smacked of Saudi interference subsequently blocked moves towards multilateral agreements for the next five years. It was not until the GCC summit in Riyadh, in December 1987, that a joint security cooperation pact was finally ratified.

The practical effects of such cooperation have included 'joint action against security offenders ... the exchange of information, training and equipment and ... the extradition of criminals'.[85] Gulf oppositionists complain that, as a result of these measures, they are at risk in all GCC states, not just their own. But the Gulf crisis has encouraged the GCC governments to strengthen such coordination. Indeed some Gulf Arabs feel this is one of the few areas in which the GCC has proved its effectiveness.

---

[80] Viorst, 'After the Liberation', p. 69.

[81] John West, 'Kuwaiti Military Vows To Be Ready Next Time', Reuters, Kuwait, 7 August 1992.

[82] Nadim Kawash, 'United Arab Emirates in Drive To Bolster Armed Forces', AFP, Abu Dhabi, 6 June 1992.

[83] In some parts of the Gulf, control of internal security is still in the hands of British (and other Western) personnel, some of whom are reminiscent of the Le Carré character who has 'hunted Communists in Malaya and Mau Mau in Kenya, Jews in Palestine, Arabs in Aden, and the Irish everywhere' – and who refers to Palestinians and Israelis as Pallies and Izzies; John Le Carré, *The Little Drummer Girl*, London, Hodder & Stoughton, 1983.

[84] Joseph Kechichian, 'The Beguiling Gulf Cooperation Council', *Third World Quarterly*, Vol. 10, No. 2, April 1988, p. 1053.

[85] Peterson, 'The GCC and Regional Security', in John Sandwick (ed.), *The Gulf Cooperation Council: Moderation and Stability in an Interdependent World,* Boulder, Colorado, Westview Press, 1987, p. 194.

9. THE END OF THE WELFARE STATE?

Social and economic development has been rapid but uneven, with sharp contrasts within and between the GCC states. While Kuwait achieved substantial literacy in a couple of decades, this has not happened in Saudi Arabia, where perhaps half the population is illiterate.[86] The kingdom has spent large sums on building schools and colleges, but calls by a number of Saudi educators for education to be made compulsory have not been heeded.

Similarly, while many Saudi cities have the latest and most expensive high-tech medicine, in villages children still suffer from such Third World diseases as malaria and bilharzia. The infant mortality rate – 65 per 1,000 in 1990 – remains high for a country with such large oil wealth and such a small population.[87] The kingdom's size (four times that of France) is not the only factor. In the 1970s and 1980s there was a mania for hospital building; but Saudi Arabia does not need more hospitals. It needs more primary health care.[88] In the city-states of the GCC, by contrast, more impressive standards have been achieved.

Throughout the GCC states, during the oil boom years from the early 1970s to the early 1980s, it looked as if the welfare state would last for ever. But since the early 1980s, the oil-producing economies have been in recession. The revenues of the thirteen OPEC producers fell from $275 billion in 1980 to a low of $77 billion in 1986, before recovering to $147 billion in 1990. This hit both rich and poor Arab states, since aid and remittances

---

[86] Birks Sinclair & Associates, *GCC Market Report 1992*, Durham, 1992, p. 92. The official figure (1991) of 62 per cent literacy is treated with caution by experts. Tayeb Saleh, a Unesco consultant and well-known Arab author, has suggested 60 per cent illiteracy; see Babakr Issa, 'Nearly Half Arab World is Illiterate', AFP, Doha, 13 March 1992.

[87] *The State of the World's Children 1992*, Oxford, OUP for Unicef, 1992. The figures for other GCC states are: Oman 37 per 1,000, Qatar 29, the UAE 24, Kuwait 17 and Bahrain 14.

[88] For a critique of health policies in the region, see Miriam Ryan, *Health Services in the Middle East*, London, Economist Intelligence Unit, 1985.

from the Gulf declined and governments were forced to face the social and political consequences of economic retrenchment.[89]

The Gulf crisis therefore added burdens to economies already in decline. It has been estimated that the crisis cost the Arab world as a whole some $620 billion. This includes the cost of infrastructure destroyed in Kuwait ($160 billion) and Iraq ($190 billion). The war itself (Desert Shield and Desert Storm) cost Arab governments $84 billion, the bulk of which was paid by Saudi Arabia and Kuwait.[90]

Saudi Arabia paid out, in direct costs, an estimated $62 billion, including $17.5 billion to the United States. The direct cost to Kuwait was some $22 billion, including $13.5 billion to the United States.[91] Indirect costs added substantially to the total. To meet the bill, the Saudi and Kuwaiti governments dug deep into their foreign reserves, announced large budget deficits and resorted to borrowing abroad. The government in Riyadh also gave the green light to big state-owned companies to borrow from foreign commercial banks. The national oil company, Saudi Aramco, arranged to borrow almost $3 billion from a group of Western and Gulf banks to help finance its expansion plans.[92]

This led economists to predict that by the end of 1992 the kingdom would have debts of some $60 billion, and that it would face debt-servicing problems by the mid-1990s unless it took determined action to cut spending or boost revenue. Evidence of such determination was lacking.[93]

These are among the short-term problems created by the war. But there are longer-term economic problems too. How can governments persuade their people that the expectations generated in the boom years are no longer realistic? If they continue to reject such measures as the introduction of income tax, how are they to increase revenue? Are they ready to kill the sacred cow of defence spending?[94] Or to break the news to their people that the end of the welfare state is nigh?

It seems they are not. A few weeks after introducing his political reforms, King Fahd cut the price of petrol, water, cooking gas and electricity.[95] The emir of Bahrain introduced similar measures shortly afterwards.[96] Such cuts defied economic logic and seemed designed to appease grumbling populations in the aftermath of the Gulf crisis.

---

[89] 'Economic Crisis in the Arab World', Overseas Development Institute, Briefing Paper, London, March 1992. Saudi revenues fell from $106 billion in 1980 to $17 billion in 1986; by 1990 they stood at $40.7 billion.

[90] Estimates from the Unified Arab Economic Report, prepared annually by the Arab League, the Arab Monetary Fund, the Arab Fund for Economic and Social Development and OAPEC; *Herald Tribune*, 8 September 1992.

[91] The total cost of the war to the United States was $57 billion, but it recovered $54 billion of this from its allies (principally Saudi Arabia, Kuwait, Germany and Japan). Reuters, Washington, 10 July 1992.

[92] Mariam Isa, 'Saudi Aramco Loans Increased to 2.9 Billion Dollars', Reuters, Manama, 5 March 1992.

[93] Mariam Isa, 'Saudi Arabia May Face Debt Service Problems', Reuters, Kuwait, 14 August 1992.

[94] By the late 1980s, the Saudi government was spending 38 times as much on defence as on health and education. Yahya Sadowski, 'Scuds versus Butter', *Middle East Report*, No. 117, July-August 1992, p. 6.

[95] *Financial Times*, 25 March 1992.

[96] *New Arabia*, May 1992.

10. CONCLUSION: FACING THE FUTURE

The Gulf crisis raised the perennial question of whether the traditional ruling families of the Arabian peninsula will survive. Five factors seem likely to be of particular importance.

THE REGIONAL DIMENSION

Regionally, the ruling families will have to find ways of coexisting with their powerful and difficult neighbours, Iraq and Iran. Achieving a stable balance of power will not be easy. The Gulf rulers fear Iraq's disintegration as much as they fear its resurgence. They are also ambivalent about Iran, seeing it as a counterweight to Iraq but fearful of its intentions not only in the Gulf but throughout the Middle East, in Central Asia and elsewhere.

 Apprehension about Iran is linked to a second factor which is unlikely to disappear, at least in the medium term: the continuing strength and influence of Islamic militancy. In the 1980s the Gulf rulers feared Iranian–backed Shi'ite subversion; in the 1990s home-grown Sunni militancy poses a more acute threat, since it challenges the legitimacy of the (Sunni) ruling families.

 Third, the GCC states – and Saudi Arabia in particular – will need to establish a modus vivendi with Yemen.

 Fourth, Gulf Arabs may be hostile to the PLO but they are not indifferent to the Arab–Israeli conflict. Many continue to be antagonistic to the Jewish state for either nationalist or religious reasons. Moreover, the success or failure of the Middle East peace process will in turn influence their relations with Washington and with the rest of the Arab world.

 Fifth, events thousands of miles away – in Algeria or Gaza or Central Asia – now have a much greater power to influence the Gulf states than in the past. This reflects not just a heightened sense of Muslim consciousness but the impact of new technology. It is estimated that there are between 16,000 and 20,000 private satellite dishes in Saudi Arabia. In Bahrain both CNN and BBC television can now be received uncensored.[97]

---

[97] *Country Reports on Human Rights Practices for 1991*, p. 1580.

OIL AND THE ECONOMY

The state of the world oil market, and hence future oil revenues, will have an obvious impact on domestic stability. In the aftermath of the Gulf war the oil producers have a common need to maximize short-term revenue. This is an interest shared by OPEC's two biggest producers, Saudi Arabia and Iran, despite their continuing mistrust and rivalry over several other issues. But a number of uncertainties surround production and price. Kuwait has gradually brought its oil production back to prewar levels, and Iraq is anxious to resume production but to do so must persuade the UN to relax or end economic sanctions. Oil and politics are as ever intertwined.[98]

Continuing recession will undoubtedly fuel grievances and increase pressure for change.

OPPOSITION GROUPS

At present there are opposition currents rather than organized, well-rooted opposition parties in the Gulf. Even in Kuwait opposition groups are weak and divided. Elsewhere oppositionists, such as Saudi and Bahraini Shi'ite groups, are active in exile but it is hard to be sure of the extent of their support and organization at home. Sunni critics of the Saudi ruling family appear to cooperate with one another and to have links with Islamic groups in other countries, but they do not have any clear structure of leadership or membership. The ruling families still have considerable power to co-opt or coerce, but over time their policies may provoke more coherent forms of opposition. There can be little doubt that at present what they fear most is the emergence of an organized and indigenous Sunni opposition.

UNITY AND COHESION

The ruling families will face perennial problems in seeking to maintain their own unity and cohesion. Such problems include the rivalry between different branches of the same family (e.g. between the Al-Ahmad and the Al-Salim branches of the Al Sabah in Kuwait); the problem of succession when, say, King Fahd or Sultan Qabus leaves the scene; and the question of whether the UAE could survive without its architect, Sheikh Zayed, currently the oldest of the six GCC rulers.

In some parts of the Gulf there are still lingering loyalties to region rather than to state. Most observers, for example, regard Sultan Qabus's efforts to integrate the southern province of Dhofar into the rest of Oman as one of his most important achievements; but the Dhofaris remain distinct, and both northerners and southerners are conscious of the distinction.[99]

In Saudi Arabia, 60 years after the kingdom's unification, differences of culture, religion and outlook remain between the Hijaz, Nejd, Asir and the Eastern Province. There is a danger that these differences might be exacerbated by continuing Sunni militancy, which both the Hijazi merchant and the Shi'ite of the Eastern Province might see as threatening – and as a reminder of Nejdi hegemony.

---

[98] For a fuller discussion of such issues see Paul Stevens, *Oil and Politics: The Post-War Gulf*, London, Royal Institute of International Affairs, October 1992.

[99] Calvin Allen, *Oman: The Modernization of the Sultanate*, Boulder, Colorado, Westview Press, 1987, pp. 121–2.

A further perennial problem is that of continuing rivalries over borders and unresolved territorial claims. The quarrel between Bahrain and Qatar over a small group of islands has flared up again recently, and has defied repeated efforts at GCC mediation.

DEMOCRACY?

Finally, the ruling families will have to decide whether to maintain their traditional system of rule or meet the challenge of political change.

King Fahd would no doubt concur with his ally King Hassan of Morocco, who recently declared that Islam prevented him from becoming a constitutional monarch.[100] The Saudi king seeks to present himself as an Islamic monarch, a term not all Muslims are happy with. (In December 1991 Saudi Arabia banned *The Economist* indefinitely for presuming to suggest that some Muslims consider monarchy un-Islamic.[101])

The king and his fellow rulers in the GCC show no inclination to turn themselves into constitutional monarchs. They do not accept that their power should be circumscribed by a system of checks and balances. The Saudi monarch is head of state, Prime Minister, head of the Council of Ministers (the cabinet) and commander of the armed forces. According to King Fahd's reforms, he will not only choose the members of his proposed *majlis*, but will also choose whether or not to accept their advice. Royal gestures – such as Fahd's decision to cut the prices of basic services and the Kuwaiti emir's to buy bad debts – show that the monarch still treats the state exchequer as his privy purse.

It is sometimes argued that the people accept the power of the ruler and the ruling family because this is the tribal tradition of Arabia. There are two possible answers to this. The first, that the system is anachronistic and should be swept away, probably convinces only a few. The more down-to-earth objection, that the system is neither very fair nor very efficient, probably convinces many more.

It is here that the traditional rulers are vulnerable. Liberals and conservatives may proffer different remedies, but they point to the same ills. Corruption, waste, inefficiency, double standards[102] are so rife that they undermine the position of the ruler and ultimately his right to rule.

Some argue that, having survived the Gulf war, the rulers can – with a little help from their friends – survive anything. This is short-sighted. The ruling families will have to change in order to survive, and change will require difficult decisions. Some see parliamentary democracy as the answer. Certainly the citizens of those states (Kuwait, Bahrain) which have had elected parliaments will not readily give them up. But elections and parliaments are not necessarily a panacea, and in any case the Gulf rulers, haunted by events in Algeria, have no intention of taking such a leap in the dark.

It is more realistic to argue for greater accountability, participation and respect for the rule of law. These things are not synonymous with democracy, but they are steps towards it.

---

[100] *Le Monde*, 2 September 1992.

[101] *The Economist*, 21 December 1991.

[102] In the Saudi case, it is not just the un-Islamic behaviour of some members of the ruling family. 'Although public theatres are still prohibited by law, private cinema and video clubs are common; although Wahhabism prohibits cigarette smoking, tobacco is subject to government taxation; and although photography is prohibited by Wahhabi teachings, photography stores are widespread.' Ayman al-Yassini, *Religion and State in the Kingdom of Saudi Arabia*, Boulder, Colorado, Westview Press, 1985, p. 117.

King Fahd, in his reforms, has accepted the principle of government accountability, but it remains to be seen whether this will have much effect. His new laws also proclaim the independence of the judiciary and the need to safeguard certain human rights, but doubts remain as to whether royal and non-royal Saudis will be treated equally before the law, and whether human rights abuses will end.

In some ways participation is the key. By announcing the creation of a *majlis*, the king has accepted the need to broaden the decision-making process, even though in practice the circle of consultation will remain narrow. However, even if the reforms are carried through, the pace of change may be too slow for a constituency which, over time, is bound to assume increasing importance: the educated young.

We do not know enough about the newly educated men and women of the Gulf, about what they think and feel, and what they want for the future. But it seems clear that for them participation means using their abilities to play a full role in society, the economy and government. At present many young Gulf Arabs feel stifled by a system which often seems to deny them such a role.[103]

> Wealth comes from connections, from wheeling and dealing, by good luck, by the regime's munificence – but not primarily because of hard work, dedication, or probity. There are few incentives for young Saudis to learn a technical skill, to become trained industrial workers, to acquire academic knowledge.... Delegation of responsibility is difficult to institute ... decisions are virtually all channelled to the top.... Loyalty is rewarded more than competence.[104]

Many qualified young people see their path blocked by older men who have been in the same positions for decades. Kuwait's foreign minister, Sheikh Sabah al-Ahmad, has had the job for almost thirty years. In Saudi Arabia, Crown Prince Abdullah has been the head of the National Guard since 1963, Prince Nayef the Minister of the Interior since 1975, Prince Salman the governor of Riyadh since 1962. The six rulers themselves have, on average, been in power for 20 years; their average age is 63.

These states are young in a double sense, since half their nationals are under 15 years of age[105] and since their feeling of nationhood is not fully formed. The Gulf crisis provoked a surge of local nationalism and alienated Gulf societies from those Arabs and other Muslims who were deemed to have given Iraq support or sympathy. But in some parts of the Gulf loyalty to family, tribe or sect remains strong. Moreover, a sense of being part of a wider Arab and Muslim world is likely to reassert itself.

How, finally, should we evaluate the impact of the Gulf crisis on the GCC states? They survived the crisis, but they can hardly be said to have survived unscathed. Operation Desert Storm cruelly exposed their triple dependence: on Western protection, on foreign workers and on a single, depletable resource. In the long run, these states cannot be strong or viable unless they shake off this dependence. One day the oil will run out. One day the patience of foreign workers may snap. One day the West will decline to come running to the rescue.

---

[103] For a portrait of the young Gulf Arab, from cradle to early employment, see Sarah Searight, 'Growing up in the Gulf', *The Middle East*, August 1985.

[104] Quandt, *Saudi Arabia in the 1980s*, pp. 91–2.

[105] Birks Sinclair & Associates, *GCC Market Report 1992*, Durham, 1992, p. 5

An American scholar has observed, 'It was a war for the status quo in the region, not an advance instalment of a "new world order".'[106] But it was a war which undermined the status quo it was designed to preserve. If the Gulf rulers and their Western allies cling to the illusion of present stability, the warning of the Gulf war will go unheeded.

---

[106] Theodore Draper, 'The True History of the Gulf War', *New York Review of Books*, 30 January 1992.

MIDDLE EAST PUBLICATIONS

Moscow and the Middle East: New Thinking on Regional Conflict
Galia Golan
Pinter/RIIA, 1992, 112pp, £8.95

Winning Peace in the Gulf: A Long-term View
Richard Dalton
RIIA Special Paper – A Middle East Programme Report
1992, 56pp, £10.00

The United Nations and the Gulf War, 1990–91: Back to the Future?
Paul Taylor and A.J.R. Groom
RIIA, Discussion Paper 38, 1992, 72pp, £5.00

Turkey and the Middle East
Philip Robins
Pinter/RIIA, 1991, 144pp, £8.95

Islam in Perspective: A Guide to Islamic Society, Politics and Law
Patrick Bannerman
Routledge, 1988, reprinted 1989, 1991, 286pp, £40.00

Islam in a World of Nation-States
James Piscatori
Cambridge University Press, 1986, 208pp, £14.95

Islam in the Political Process
Edited by James Piscatori
Cambridge University Press, 1983, 250pp, £13.95

Europe and the Arab World: Discord or Symbiosis?
David McDowall
RIIA Special Paper - A Middle East Programme Report
European Community and the Arab World series
1992, 42pp, £10.00

Oil and Politics: The Post War Gulf
Paul Stevens
RIIA Special Paper – A Middle East Programme Report
1992, 36pp, 3 tables, 5 figures, £10.00

FORTHCOMING PUBLICATIONS

Kuwait and Iraq: Historical Claims and Territorial Disputes
Richard Schofield

This study explains the emergence and development of the territorial dispute. In so doing it tells the story of the emergence of the modern states, and gives graphic insight into the haphazard nature of the boundary demarcation process. In this second edition Richard Schofield has incorporated developments in the post-Gulf Crisis period, including the work and conclusions of the UN Commission established after the conflict to look into the border demarcation issue.

RIIA Special Paper – A Middle East Programme Report
Second edition available January 1993, 200pp, 13 maps, £10.00

Whither Israel?
This collection of edited works by eleven eminent Israeli academics and experts focuses on the changes taking place inside Israeli society and seeks to judge the impact that this is likely to have on policymaking in the future. The book comprises three sections: Israeli Political System, Issues in Israeli Society, and Challenges and Reform. A number of highly topical issues such as the influx of Soviet immigrants and the loyalty of the Israeli Arab population are covered.

Keith Kyle and Joel Peters (eds)
RIIA/I.B. Tauris, available spring 1993

EC–Arab World Economic Relations
This report analyses the economic relationship between the European Community and the Arab World. It examines recent and current trends in economic ties, with particular attention to trade, aid and investment. It concludes by describing the current challenges, and the prospects for enhancing the relationship.

RIIA Special Paper – A Middle East Programme Report
Mina Toksoz, available March 1993